Transformation of Cryptograpny

Transformation of Cryptography

Fundamental concepts of Encryption, Milestones, Mega-Trends and sustainable Change in regard to Secret Communications and its Nomenclatura

Linda A. Bertram & Gunther van Dooble

Impressum

Bertram, Linda A. / Dooble, Gunther van: Transformation of Cryptography - Fundamental concepts of Encryption, Milestones, Mega-Trends and sustainable Change in regard to Secret Communications and its Nomenclatura, Norderstedt 2019,
ISBN: 9783749450749.

This essay has been published first in the book: Nomenclatura – Encyclopedia of modern Cryptography and Internet Security, 2019.

Manufacturer / Publisher / Printing:
BoD - Books on Demand, Norderstedt - http://www.bod.de
More bibliographic info under: https://portal.dnb.de

9 783749 450749

Mathematicians and computer scientists have the human right to privacy in their hand through a calculation of the truth.

Transformation of Cryptography

Fundamental concepts of Encryption, Milestones, Mega-Trends and sustainable Change in regard to Secret Communications and its Nomenclatura

by Linda A. Bertram & Gunther van Dooble

Until now, the creation, application, and research of cryptography and its algorithms and processes as well as the programming of corresponding software were reserved for state institutions, subject matter experts, and the military.

In the recent past, in addition to the centuries-old encryption with a secret key, the encryption with a key pair - consisting of a public and a private key - has been established.

In this case, by means of mathematical calculation (a prime factor decomposition) with the public key of the communication partner and the own keys, a message can be correspondingly encrypted and decrypted again.

It is an encryption not with a shared secret, but with a so-called "Public Key Infrastructure (PKI)"(↗ [02][16][25][44] [39]): Just the pair of keys, one of which can be public - and the other, which is private.

Since then, these two methods of encryption exist: The method of using a secret key is known as symmetric encryption (↗[54][21][15][04][01]) (both communication partners must know the password) and PKI encryption with a public and a private key is known as asymmetric encryption.

The description of the transmission of a symmetric credential in asymmetric encryption - without any major security concerns - was a milestone in cryptography.

Since then, modern cryptography has evolved steadily. Today, mathematical knowledge has greatly expanded with respect to the field of cryptography. Process-oriented, breathtaking concepts and inventions that have brought the protection of texts – our written communication – further forward and made it safer have also been discovered.

In the following, we want to highlight and summarize more than two dozen fundamental concepts, milestones, mega-trends, and sustainable changes to secure online communication and encryption that also provide a foundation for the need to teach with a modern Encyclopedia of Cryptography (↗[56]).

The heyday of "end-to-end encryption" (1)

The conversion to respective supplementation of point-to-point encryption with end-to-end encryption (↗[24]) has not only been carried out technically, but also in common language use: both encryption routes (point-to-point as well as end-to-end) have been present structurally, however, the awareness of end-to-end encryption has become increasingly important as Internet and mobile communications began to become more and more intercepted at the beginning of the 21st century.

Everyone today speaks of end-to-end encryption. Yes, "end-to-end encryption" is even used by many citizens as a term for "encryption" itself. We ask ourselves today if the connection between you and I is also completely encrypted, that is, completely encrypted from my end to your end, and thus without any gaps.

Because, a point-to-point encryption in e-mail and chat – such as with the well-known XMPP-chat (↗[61][32]) – means that the user to the server has transport encryption. The server can read the data, and then encrypt it before sending it again point-to-point (transport) encrypted.

This also shows that legacy chat protocols or transport encryption were designed at the time and that the corresponding applications today have architectural problems due to the lack of programming of (continuous) end-to-end encryption - or at least make efforts to fill these gaps.

End-to-end encryption often needs to be requested or prescribed and installed later.

For example, XMPP has released a manifest for encryption (↗[61]), but only a few clients and servers have improved their content and code so far.

There remain questions about a fragmented IT architecture as well as questions about the content quality standard: whether all modern possibilities can be elaborated in the lowest common denominator.

That means that the newer developments - firstly to equip the clients based on the algorithm RSA (↗[12][52]) with alternative algorithms such as NTRU (↗[36][67][11][23]) and McEliece (↗[50][06][20][51]), and secondly the option of a quick and frequent exchange of end-to-end keys - were postponed into one by the manifest undefined future.

In an IT landscape of numerous clients and servers, this requires considerable programming effort or, consequently, the exclusion of plain text on each forwarding server: If you wanted to disable all XMPP messengers with RSA encryption, and you would want to ban all servers to forward plaintexts - so they follow the end-to-end paradigm consistently - XMPP would be in a desolate state, as the infrastructure often could not achieve this quality and security status.

The manifesto remained gentle and predicted little: "This commitment to encrypted connections is only the first step ... and does not obviate the need for technologies supporting end-to-end encryption (such as Off-the-Record Messaging or OTR (↗[31]), strong authentication, channel binding, secure DNS, server identity checking, and secure service delegation" (↗[61]).

To „not obviate supporting end-to-end encryption in XMPP" (ibid), does not mean to make it good practice or even mandatory.

XMPP thus remains - despite the pleasant standardization in the area - in terms of encryption, a dinosaur, which is best corrected for security reasons, because the common or even modern standard in terms of cryptographic processes is not achieved here.

Anyone who has grown up with plaintext-XMPP will possibly defend the well-known with high emotions and the cryptographical development - for example, that today is referred to further developed end-to-end encryption - becomes a crypto-war, if not a religious community-war, that ignites on developers, who have not yet been able to code-out the plaintext capabilities of servers.

For example, in his FOSS-ASIA presentation in 2018, Daniel Gultsch lists 8 out of 30 popular XMPP servers without XEP-0384 OMEMO (↗[28][69]) encryption with the comment: "The problem of the fragmented Ecosystem XMPP is that it has outdated servers, which don't support those latest encrypting extensions. Part of the Solution is to make the problem visible" (↗[32]).

The conversion of this architecture and infrastructure to native and end-to-end encryption is not yet, at least years after the encryption manifest, in the best garb of good practice, as it was the case with the more promising XMPP-servers Prosody and Ejabberd.

However, the evolution of end-to-end encryption in other messengers and in IT in general now clearly shows that the paradigm of end-to-end encryption has become a predicate value, which sets secure encryption - without a third party reading in the middle - as a standard.

If a (at that time) de facto communication standard such as XMPP calls all - servers, as well as clients, e.g. to implement higher standards or even end-to-end encryption, and the implementation is still not sustainable, at least as long there is room for further activities and instances without encryption are not turned off, this shows not only the fragmented state with respect to antiquated standards, but at the same time a heyday of end-to-end encryption, which is on everyone's agenda today.

And thus, old standards with this new standard outdates or stimulates the comprehensive revision with further steps because the end-to-end encryption has evolved itself, as follows:

Manifesting End-to-End Encryption in „Cryptographic Calling" (2)

In many cases, encryption software has one encryption key per online session. As an example, the OTR encryption (a forerunner of OMEMO encryption) can be considered: Again, one key per session was sent.

However, more advanced programming can now send any number of temporary keys per online session through a secure channel. This is called Cryptographic Calling (↗[30][23]).

Secure communication with a friend has thus become convenient, as we know from a telephone call: pick up and call the handset, and end the session after or in the middle of a conversation by putting the handset back on its hook. Respectively for the smartphone generation: the conversation is ended with the push of a button. Regardless of the duration of each online session, especially on always-on devices.

Another criteria was that the previous session orientation changed into a generation of end-to-end encryption at any time. Forward Secrecy (↗[14][23]), meaning the use of temporary end-to-end encrypting keys, went into serial production with key generation. It broke out of congruence with the session.

Instant Perfect Forward Secrecy (IPFS) (3)

Cryptographic Calling meant that a time frame was no longer bound to sessions, but a user could execute a "Cryptographic Call" "at any time" and "immediately" and renew the temporary, end-to-end encrypting keys.

Perfect Forward Secrecy - that is, protection by temporary keys - has become "instant": security has been implemented for immediate application and renewal, hence the term: Instant Perfect Forward Secrecy (IPFS) (↗[23]).

The Melodica Button (4)

In this context, another term emerged in the application world: The term "Multi-Encrypted-Long-Distance-Calling". Alone in its abbreviation "MELODICA" it is already indicated that with end-to-end encryption should be played nimble and fast, it must be renewable at any time, much like a musician plays the keys on a musical instrument.

MELODICA (↗[56]) was a button that allowed users to automatically renew the end-to-end encryption by pressing a button: The MELODICA button was built into the UI of Crypto Messenger GoldBug (↗[03][42][59][22][72][08][34]) as a graphical element for the Instant Perfect Forward Secrecy (IPFS) process described above and logically the icon represented a piano keyboard with white and black keys.

When pressed, new symmetric keys are transferred for temporary purposes through a permanent secure channel to open a new temporary communication channel. However, the button disappeared with the elaboration of the various other methodological types of Cryptographic Calling.

Cryptographic Calling was first programmed into the Encryption Suite "Spot-On" (↗[66][23][30][65]) in 2013 and then continuously elaborated and further developed. Today, different methodological types of Cryptographic Calling can be distinguished.

Elaboration of the methodical types of Cryptographic Calling (5)

More important than being able to renew the end-to-end encryption multiple times during a session (making it very difficult for attackers to succeed in attempting to catch or find end-to-end encrypting keys), was the fact that methodically could now be played with the existing hybrid encryption and Multi-Encryption.

The secure channel for transmitting temporary keys could be both symmetrical and asymmetrical.

And now, in the asymmetric channel, either a symmetric key could be used for the temporary forward-secrecy key, or a temporary asymmetric public key could be used.

The same was due of course vice versa for a symmetrically-encrypted channel. And thirdly, the temporary key no longer needs to be sent through the permanent key channel, but can also be sent through a secure channel of an existing (previous) temporary key.

For example: An (asymmetric) temporary key follows a (symmetric) temporary key. With the Spot-On-Encryption Suite, which established the Cryptographic Calling, therefore, at the same time a quasi birth - at least one hour of enrollment – of the programmed Multi-Encryption (↗[26][23][22][49]) was given:

No other encryption program encrypted messages multiple times at this time and was able to send the new temporary keys so varied and instant.

The various types of Cryptographic Calling joined the now historic MELODICA button, as there were now more than a handful of possible ways and variants of calling, as the linked references further elaborate (↗[30][23]).

With Cryptographic Calling, (possibly already multiple) encryption received another encryption layer.

Multi-Encryption (6)

Applied programming of hybrid encryption (means in the end that different variants are used at the same time or one after the other) finally led this theoretical and so far little-studied concept of Multi-Encryption with its variety of options into practical application processes.

It is with the Multi-Encryption not only about encrypting a ciphertext again. It's also about possibly changing the algorithm of encryption in the second round.

While an algorithm knows several rounds, operations, repetitions of e.g. substitutions, multi-encryption now puts a whole new dimension on top of it: If Plaintext has been converted to a ciphertext with the RSA algorithm, and this is then converted to another ciphertext by the McEliece algorithm: What comes out at the end? And can this be better or worse analyzed using the usual methods of cryptanalysis (↗[62][07][43][29])?

It is no longer just a question of substituting individual characters, but a completely new algorithm is applied to the ciphertext end product of a previously used algorithm.

Multi-Encryption thus consists of three main areas: The multiple encryption (conversion from ciphertext to ciphertext), and secondly, a mixture of algorithms, to thirdly the mixture of methods; which could certainly also fall under algorithms, therefore we say: Process chains: The mixture also of the transfer ways of the keys, for example, complements methodically and procedurally the mixture of algorithms, because it is a difference whether RSA-AES-McEliece triple changed ciphertext is sent through a channel of a permanent key or is sent through the channel of a temporary key.

Multi-Encryption has become the mega-topic of current cryptography and its analysis through this applied programming and conceptual elaboration; and was named as a research area in many online portals and forums like Reddit and others - more than ever before on the agenda.

Further research will be dedicated to these three aspects of multi-coding, as this new quality may also reveal security gaps or vulnerabilities of certain algorithms.

As an example: Is ciphertext, which has been converted three times with RSA-AES-McEliece, more meaningful in reference to a plain text than a just one-time RSA-only converted plaintext to ciphertext? Or in the comparison of three times with RSA converted plaintext? Respectively is three times RSA-converted text less secure than a three times McEliece-converted text?

Of course, Multi-Encryption is also associated with interests at the owners of existing solutions, definitions and processes, if the structure could be strengthened or weakened by an algorithm, if ciphertext is again converted to ciphertext by a (further) algorithm.

The applications which up to now use Multi-Encryption assume that the encryption becomes particularly secure if ciphertext is repeated for another conversion to ciphertext, e.g. if it is encrypted symmetrically and then sent through a TLS($\nearrow$[53]) channel. For the reverse conversion from ciphertext to ciphertext in several rounds, additional security must therefore be assumed -

until dedicated research studies could indicate otherwise. Anything else would be illogical assumptions, because: Double-encrypted is better.

Multi-Encryption requires programming knowledge from mathematicians (7)

Combinatorics can no longer refer to the application of only one procedure from a discipline, but integrates hybrid and multiple up to exponential processes from different disciplines. The practice and theory of encryption is complete, if, in addition to mathematics and combinatorics also applied programming is added, as well as: If network theory, graph theory, and other departments are supplemented.

Cascading and Multiple Encryption is not only a young field of research, but gets and finds significant boost and complementary additions in all these neighboring disciplines. If you want to deal with encryption in the future, at least together with your team one should also be able to program appropriate software for Multi-Encryption and the mathematical algorithms in one of the popular developer languages: Mathematical calculations have to be supplemented by the knowledge of applied software programming in order to be able to obtain the resulting ciphertext by the computer-aided calculations.

REPLEO (8)

In the centuries-old symmetric encryption with a password or an known algorithm, which reverses the letters or characters, the key may under no circumstances be revealed – also according to the well-known Kerkhoffs's principle (↗[45]) - that states, that not the algorithm should be protected, but in particular the key.

Indeed, Kerkhoffs lived at a time when there was still no asymmetric encryption existing with PKI respectively a private and public key. But what if this principle would be also applied to asymmetric encryption? Anyone here would say that the "public key" does not mean "public key" for nothing? - It can be made public. However, it is though technically possible, as soon as I have received the public key of a friend, to convert my own public key - before sending it - with this, their public key to ciphertext. This is called REPLEO (↗[23]) and protects the public key.

The Kerkhoffs's principle referred to asymmetric encryption - aka titled "Kerkhoffs's principle of asymmetry" - is thus a REPLEO, which also encodes and protects the public key of PKI at a transfer of the key.

But this is not yet a solution to the key transport problem - which is essentially in the symmetric encryption with a passphrase – instead it is only a protection of the public key of asymmetric encryption, for those who do not want to make this public key public to everyone.

But how can a symmetric key, a secret passphrase, be securely transmitted over the Internet? By sending it over a secure channel. One possible method dedicated to this question was given with a so-called EPKS channel.

The EPKS-Method (9)

Symmetric keys - e.g. a passphrase - can be securely transmitted between two nodes on the Internet using an EPKS-channel (↗[23][56]). The EPKS-channel allows to send the key over this channel. And channel message recipients have then automatically integrated the key into their instance, and could use this key to further decode messages.

The EPKS-channel was first integrated also in the above-mentioned Encryption Suite, as it was one of the early comprehensive software that sent keys through encrypted channels, which in turn could be then used as an own encrypted channel.

It is implemented there in such a way for any content or purpose, however, it was integrated for the transmission of URLs or own bookmarks from a URL database to a friend or circle of friends as a default template (URL Community).

The automated transmission and integration of keys over the EPKS-channel was presented as a model of secure key transmission with this concept capture and programming within the so-called Echo Protocol (↗[30]): Echo Public Key Sharing (EPKS).

AutoCrypt (10)

In derivative applications, concepts of automated key transfer and key integration of EPKS have been deduced, e.g. also integrated under the name AutoCrypt (↗[56]) in various e-mail and chat applications. At the beginning, two e-mail users exchange an e-mail that ensures that both users can swap their public PKI key. If this is the case, the keys are exchanged and all other e-mails are continuously encrypted with the public key.

Reading State-of-the-Art Signals: Fiasco Forwarding with Fiasco Keys (11)

Thus, when a subscriber resends with old traditional messengers after a received message again for the first time, he / she renews the session key material again by a so-called Diffie-Hellman key exchange (asymmetric key), in which e.g. its own new key is combined with the already-known key of the remote station (D/H-Ratchet (↗[19])).

In this Ratchet method, symmetric keys are derived from the session key material using a key derivation function. Since the key derivation function is based on a hash function, this step is called a hash ratchet. For each message, the protocol relays one of two hash ratchets (one to send, one to receive) initialized based on a shared secret from a D/H-Ratchet.

At the same time, it tries to provide the remote station with a new public DH value at each opportunity and to push on its own local DH ratchet each time a new public DH value arrives from the remote station. This method has been incorporated in numerous known commercial messengers (such as WhatsApp).

Security experts see weaknesses here, when in commercial or even proprietary products no own server can be used. In addition, the schematic consequence of "pushing on" the keys is considered a special vulnerability: If a key is in a defined location, it is also easy to find.

And: Keys are still being exchanged, which could be derived using a zero-knowledge-proof-method (↗[09][05][60]) without exchanging the key.

After all, why not create and send a dozen keys per chat message that are collected in a pool and are all tried out, from the most recent to the oldest, per received message? Or also create (symmetric) keys that are formed according to a two-way calling (↗[30][23]) by both sides, in which each communication partner contributes 50% in the generation and exchange of the secret, symmetric password in this type of Cryptographic Calling? Fifty-Fifty as a method in the formation of common keys.

This further method of sending numerous keys - besides two-way calling - is called Fiasco Forwarding (↗[63][30]) with corresponding Fiasco Keys (ibid) and was first developed in the Smoke Messenger (↗ [63][64]) as Java code.

Although this messenger is not commercially distributed and therefore less popular, it is on the protocol level, a fuller and more secure security-design than the previous mentioned Signal Protocol for end-to-end encryption with a Ratchet method, which also inserts no manual and individual Cryptographic Calling (end-to-end encryption with user-defined passphrases), do not allow the use of easy-to-administer own servers and even is not open source when using popular communication servers.

So anyone who turns the Signal (↗[47][13]) Protocol - as this schematic Ratchet method is now called - in the sense of mobile encryption as state of the art, is no longer up to date: The extremely volatile design using Fiasco keys or a Fiasco Forwarding has significant advantages over other, more schematic protocol implementations.

With these innovations - REPLEO such as EPKS or the derivative AutoCrypts - on issues of the key transport problem, the key transmission is only better protected with a further layer of security respectively (at AutoCrypt) more convenient for the user only through automated key acceptance.

However, Fiasco Forwarding with its Fiasco Keys multiplies the number of keys in advance and further develops schematic procedures with so far only one key per message, so that one can speak of a Volatile Encryption ($\nearrow$[56]).

Volatile does not mean that encryption is shaky and uncertain, but volatile encryption refers to unsteady and temporary keys that are fluctuating, volatile, and evaporating - thus reducing the chance of decryption by multiplying the amount of decryption attempts required per message.

A fundamental innovation in terms of key transmission and risks is the innovation of the Secret Streams and Juggerknot Keys. The key is no longer transmitted via the Internet, but mathematically and methodically formed and derived on each side.

The third Epoch of Cryptography: Solving the key transport problem as another innovative breakthrough in cryptography? (12)

As has been the case, the passing on of a symmetric key - a passphrase - to the communication partner constituted until recently a security-relevant problem and a central aspect of the analysis in order to decrypt cryptography, or to gain insights for it.

Another innovative breakthrough in cryptography was given with another step in the solution of the key transport problem, which was evidenced by the two concepts and programmed procedures "Secret Streams" (↗[23]) and "Juggerknot Keys" (↗[63]).

With that, two communication partners can communicate encrypted with each other via Internet infrastructure, without having to transfer the current key via the Internet. These potentials offer epochal changes in cryptography.

Because the application of a zero-knowledge proof for the derivation of keys on both sides of the communication partners from a common unspoken level of knowledge, the external is not obvious, is not only mathematically brilliant, but also represents a groundbreaking development in cryptography in this process design when the well-known key transport problem experiences these various innovative solution perspectives.

Let's describe each innovation in this new direction in turn:

Cesura in Cryptography: Secret Streams (13)

Secret Streams denote the creation of numerous temporary keys, that are in the build process derived from a not-over-the-network transmitted passphrase. The keys come or derive out of a Socialist Millionaire Process (SMP) (↗[74][10][03][66]).

In this process, both friends enter a secret password in their client - and this is not transmitted over the Internet. Using a mathematical method, a zero-knowledge proof, it is determined whether the same password has been entered on both sides.

The so-called Socialist Millionaire Protocol produces the mathematical calculation of this Zero-Knowledge Proof.

The Socialist Millionaire Problem is one in which two millionaires want to determine if their wealth is equal without disclosing any information about their riches to each other. It is a variant of the Millionaire's Problem whereby two millionaires wish to compare their riches to determine who has the most wealth without disclosing any information about their riches to each other.

If the mathematical SMP proof is successful, it can be assumed that both communication participants have entered the same password into the mathematical process in each of their clients - without, however, that this password has ever been transmitted over the Internet.

This method of the Secret Streams, which until now has only been used in two programmings, as well as the Juggerknot Keys ($\nearrow$[63]) might therefore be regarded as further milestones - if not even as the beginnings of a possible new epoch - in cryptography: While we have just seen above that end-to-end encryption is currently experiencing its popular heyday, this flowering has long been outdated by this cryptographic design: passwords encrypting end-to-end no longer have to be transmitted over the Internet!

It certainly needs furthermore secure channels, but there is no need to transfer a key online over these channels - as it was the case when sending a symmetric key.

While the PKI as a "new direction" has become modern with the secure transmission of the key in the Diffie-Hellmann exchange ($\nearrow$[19]), today it is also for the symmetric encryption pointed out that - thanks to this "new direction" Secret Streams - no symmetric key must be transmitted anymore over the network from one end to the other end.

Secret Streams can be another big step in cryptography following the invention of asymmetric encryption, solving the key transport problem and eliminating Kerkhoffs' principle.

Thus, Secret Streams could also be discussed as Kerkhoff's Principle Number 2, as a dialectical reference function of Kerkhoffs's Principle, or even as Kerkhoffs's Inversion.

Of course, both communication partners first have to discuss a common level of knowledge or experience with minimal communication: e.g. in advance in real life.

In the way: Can you still remember the name of the restaurant in which we met? Please enter this name as a phrase in the communication client.

The phrase is not transmitted over the Internet, but the mathematical calculation of the zero-knowledge proof shows us whether we both entered the identical passphrase; and we too are authentic persons. Then numerous temporary keys are derived identically on each side by the method / function of the Secret Streams.

Secret Streams are programmed in C ++ and were first developed in the popular and already named Encryption Suite Spot-On.

They offer potential to dispense with the transmission of keys in secure and unsecured channels of the Internet.

Cesura in Cryptography: Juggerknot Keys (14)

An elimination of the key transport problem is also found in the Juggerknot Keys. These are exemplary programmed in Java (in the application of the Crypto Chat Messenger Smoke (↗[63]) for the Android operating system) and build on a similar method of a Zero-Knowledge Proof: With the difference that here not a (Socialist-Millionaire) SMP process was used, but the mathematically-similar process of the Juggernaut PAKE Protocols (↗[33]), in which both communication partners - each on the own side - also enter a secret phrase, which in turn is again not shared over the Internet. Then, temporary end-to-end encrypting keys are derived.

Also here it can be spoken not only of a mathematically-stunning process, but also of an innovation in cryptography: Encryption without a critical transfer of the key over the Internet.

After symmetric encryption, the establishment of asymmetric encryption and now the solution of the key transport problem with zero-knowledge proofs with derivative keys, this third epoch of cryptography is not only a new descriptor for theoretical cryptography, but also a model for programmers in their applied development, since the open source programming in both major programming languages (C++ and Java) are available as software libraries.

Now you might want to consider that you have to exchange a secret before using the online Internet infrastructure, so this is only partially correct, because it is about picking up a keyword from a common pool of experience, without naming this keyword. Ultimately, in the simple case, each communication partner is indexed or mapped only once with an alias, and henceforth, encryption can take place without the transfer of keys over the Internet - each with freshly derived keys.

So, if the British agent knows that he has to mentally map his friend, the American agent, with the password "Houston," and the Russian agents with the password "Moscow" and the Chinese agents with the password "Beijing," then they need in the third epoch of cryptography no key exchange anymore, but only a messenger and appropriate network or Internet architecture (i.e. an online connection) to communicate undisturbed. When the British agent talks to the American agent, they both enter the phrase "Houston".

Transferring current (fresh) keys over the Internet is no longer necessary; they are derived from the remembered agreement of both communication partners, which only need to be agreed once and then mathematically proved – that means at the same time, the communication partner is also authenticated - but can henceforth communicate under the paradigm of "Instant Perfect Forward Secrecy" (IPFS).

The solution of the key transport system by means of Secret Streams and Juggerknot Keys, in which the symmetric key on both sides are formed by a mathematical zero-knowledge process and therefore no longer have to be transmitted over one channel, defines a new perspective for programming and the further future in cryptography.

Machine learning using cryptographic tokens - using the example of the Adaptive Echo (15)

Using cryptographic tokens not only machines in the network can be controlled, but also paths can be defined according to a graph design in the network. As an example, the elaboration of the Adaptive Echo (↗[30]) may be mentioned, in which a connected node excludes by means of a cryptographic token that another connected node receives a certain information.

The uninformed node does not even know that its connected network environment is denying it a particular message.

This would be comparable to a historical example in the analogue world, as if in August 1941 Admiral Kimmel had been deprived of "Security Reasons" (↗[58]) as well as Pearl Harbor itself highly significant news related to the port and the fleet, and the Japanese apparently did not send the messages - or at that time the decoding codes - anymore.

In today's digital network, machines and nodes therefore learn when they receive information, or else they receive no information. Adaptive protocols are therefore to be combined with an Environmental Learning.

"Machine Learning" has become "Environmental Learning" because the context of all machines in the network has to be considered when neighbor machines learn by not including their own machine in the learning process of others.

Adaptive protocols such as the aforementioned AE Protocol give us the opportunity to modernize and refine the terms and content - as it is comparable the case with: "good practice" rather than "best practice" and "extra-occupational learning" rather than "lifelong learning", or "Work-Life-Learn-Balance" instead of "Work-Life-Balance". And here: "Environmental Learning" instead of "Machine Learning".

While the Borg collective known from the Star Trek films assimilates and alters new entities, environmental learning deals with exactly the reverse process: extracting a node from the flow of information, so that other machines have a knowledge leap or information advantage, and learn accordingly and the assignment of rights for a neighbor machine is defined. Thus, by means of Cryptographic Tokens (↗[23]) and adaptive protocols (such as the AE protocol), a machine – and also often human beings – can only collect the information that is also made available to them.

This leads to the process of Cryptographic Discovery (↗[66][30]). These are "discovery processes" that use cryptographic values in a network landscape. Machine Learning has expanded into Environmental Learning and will then merge into an encrypted environment in the concept of Cryptographic Discovery:

Cryptographic Discovery (16)

The concept of Cryptographic Discovery can be understood in the sense of a Distributed Hash Table (DHT) (↗[73]), which further develops it.

A DHT is a data structure that can be used, for example, to record the location of a file in a P2P system. The data is distributed as evenly as possible over all existing storage nodes. Each storage node corresponds to an entry in the hash table. The self-organizing data structure can thus map the failure, accession and exit of nodes. However, this carries security risks: each node knows the address and memory content of all other nodes.

In the concept of Cryptographic Discovery information is now passed on the basis of cryptographic tokens, so that a server can collect information about its environment, in particular via a graph to be controlled to reach the destination, without having to directly index or know the target itself.

For example, if a server receives the information that Alice can be reached through Bob, it does not have to send information to Alice over the route of Ed or Maria. This concept is based on Machine Learning - or, as we have learned, better: Environmental Learning - through cryptographic tokens, as found, for example, in said adaptive protocol. Cryptographic Discovery will therefore need further research in this regard. This concept paper of the communication server SmokeStack (↗[64]) was also used there for pre-programmed processing, which has to be taken up further in terms of information-theoretical analysis as well as with regard to analysis of the program code as a research topic.

This process was bundled in the neatly-worded "Beyond Cryptographic Routing" (↗ [30]). It is no longer just about replacing the IP address with a cryptographic value that has been formed, be it through a cryptographic hash function or through a public cryptographic key. But it is about that routing in a "flooding network" or better: "mesh network" (↗[35]) is basically target-less, so we can no longer speak of routing. The "New Direction" is: Some also have "No Direction". Complex chaos. Therefore "Beyond Routing". This has become analyzable and describable from the Echo Protocol (↗[30][23]) published since the first decade of the 21st century.

Beyond Cryptographic Routing: The Echo Protocol (17)

The Echo is a protocol that has been established for many years and is implemented in various applications as well as servers for encryption and network design. It creates a flooding or mesh network with its basic rule that the encrypted packets are forwarded to all connected nodes. As with an acoustic echo, all can hear the echo after sending the signal.

It can also be compared to dolphin communication: each dolphin sends out a signal to be picked up and processed by any dolphins surrounding it. Each node that is connected, or any dolphin that can receive the signal or message packet, will process it.

Each node is also a simple reflector in the echo protocol, because every packet that comes in is also sent out again.

Finally, every sent packet in the Echo protocol is always encrypted. And: It can also be Multi-Encryption. Not only is the flooding character freer from data retention analysis (with their meta-data to: Who sends when to whom?), But because it carries the character of "Beyond Cryptographic Routing", there is in the analysis no destination address assignable.

Encryption occurs at three possible levels: First, the encrypted packet is secured with asymmetric encryption, that means the public key of the communication partner is used. Furthermore, the message itself can be e.g. encrypted by means of the Cryptographic Calling symmmetric (with a passphrase) and thirdly, this packet is sent through an SSL/TLS-secured (self-signed) channel to the communication partner.

These potentials, which develop when Multi-Encryption and Graph Theory combine, offer a whole new paradigm and high-quality, further research content with this now in numerous clients such as Spot-On, GoldBug, FireFloo, Smoke Messenger, and Smokestack Server Software built-in and well-documented encryption protocol (ibid).

In addition to the three layers of encryption and the two basic features of the protocol (fundamental encryption and fundamental shipping to all connected neighbors), a third and further feature of the Echo protocol is an independent innovation and a milestone in cryptography: The characteristics of the Echo-Matches. Because this increases the security of encrypted communication in networks centrally. So why is the echo destination-free and sender-free and therefore particularly secure? The cryptographic Echo-Match shows it as follows:

The Echo-Match (18)

The Echo-Match (↗[30]) is the core idea of the Echo: The plaintext of the message is hashed and the hash is appended to the ciphertext as encrypted capsule.

If a recipient with the stored keys of their friends can reconvert the ciphertext to plaintext, and the hash of the ciphertext matches the supplied hash, the message has been successfully decoded with this right key and will be delivered.

Since the hash of the ciphertext message is not invertible and there is no information about the plaintext, it can be safely enclosed. The hash comparisons before decryption attempts of the encrypted echo capsule are then called an Echo-Match.

A successful Echo-Match decides whether the message is displayed in its own client.

The echo match is designed by the supplemental Vapor Protocol (↗[66][56]) to follow the logic of the TCP protocol (↗[37][68]), that means, if an encrypted capsule in a node has been successfully read, a message is returned to the sender again as an acknowledgment.

This can be used to replace the TCP protocol with the Vapor protocol based on the Echo and the

Echo-Match, when it comes to creating a completely encrypted network communication, which nevertheless takes place destination-and-sender-free and due to the match-check remains sovereign on your own machine in localhost.

Exponential Encryption: The amalgamation of graph theory with encryption (19)

Combining the just-presented way of multiple encryption with the graph theory, derives from the principle of the Echo Protocol (that each encrypted message is to be sent to all connected nodes) - a multiplying, even Exponential Encryption (↗[30]).

It is reminiscent of the historical example of rice grains on a chess board field that doubles with every other field on the chessboard. So-called Congestion Control (↗ [38][27]) filters out once processed messages in a node again and relieves the CPU, if a message has already been forwarded and should be forwarded on the chaotic use of the graphs to a node a second time.

The POPTASTIC-Protocol: Chat over E-Mail (20)

Encrypted messages have harmonized e-mails and chats in the common term Messages. Why should you look at e-mails and chats differently? So on the technical level logically with the POPTASTIC protocol chat also over E-Mail servers like POP3 and IMAP was made possible.

This has been published in 2014 in the Spot-On Kernel as a concept and as programmed code in the messengers Spot-On as well as the GoldBug Messenger.

It was not only described in detail in the project documentation, but also analyzed in detail in the Big Seven study by auditors (↗[03]). Since then, numerous mobile clients such as Delta Chat, Ox Talk, Lettera, and Spike (↗[56]) have used and developed the POPTASTIC protocol for encrypted chat over email servers in addition to GoldBug and Spot-On.

Since email servers are available everywhere as an infrastructure, the POPTASTIC chat over email has also solved the server issue in communications applications and put them on a broad footing. This not only offers maximum potential in terms of availability, but also in terms of technical-content for further designs as follows:

FileSharing & Turtle Hopping over POPTASTIC (21)

FileSharing must also be encrypted nowadays. Due to the concern about the sharing of copyrighted content, no peer-to-peer networks can be made (if the peer would be an attacker), but must be encrypted done as friend-to-friend in the sense of a web-of-trust. This is always available via the infrastructure of a POPASTIC Protocol (↗[46][30])! Now, when sharing and searching files over the network is made by friends of friends, this is based on the idea of the Turtle Hopping Protocol (↗[57]48]).

In other words, if file sharing with turtle hopping is now implemented on the basis of the POPTASTIC protocol in one of the above-mentioned clients, the concept would have been transferred to mobile devices, just like the desktop application RetroShare (↗[42]) as one of the few encrypting file-sharing applications.

This is an interesting perspective not only in terms of ideological and technical, but also in terms of law, when a turtle hopping is based on the POPTASTIC protocol and realized in a programmed mobile client, as the authors Gasakis / Schmidt first described as a concept "The POPTASTIC Echo Turtle" (↗[30:67]).

It projects the existing Web-of-Trust application RetroShare for the desktop only mobile and via given e-mail servers. Because of encryption and available e-mail servers, such programming offers potential to become the new distributed computing model of F2F Crypto-Torrents (↗[56]) in a distributed system or network.

Establishment of sovereign concepts (22)

Another trend has been the possibility of having own public asymmetric keys with external providers e.g. a cloud (Customer Supplied Encryption Keys, CSEK (↗[40]) or end-to-end encryption with own passwords) on both sides. Users can define their own compositions in terms of values for a Crypto-DNA (↗[56]) or for a key-gertgaegasergeneration in modern software.

The Age of Quantum Computers: A New Life Cycle with the McEliece Algorithm and the McNoodle Library (23)

On the one hand we have to change the pure mathematical calculation from the insecure algorithms to the safe algorithms for the age of quantum computing.

A prominent example is the product lifecycle of the RSA algorithm, which is gradually reaching retirement age, and with new algorithms such as McEliece and NTRU is considering adding not only a supplement, but also a necessary replacement of itself: Since the algorithm RSA is now considered to be insecure after official announcement by the American Institute NIST in 2016 (↗[55]), because the underlying mathematical method of prime factor decomposition can be broken by fast quantum computers, other algorithms such as NTRU or McEliece need to be used.

The NIST writes: „RSA Public key Signatures, key establishment: No longer secure. ECDSA, ECDH (Elliptic Curve Cryptography) Public key Signatures, key exchange: No longer secure. DSA (Finite Field Cryptography) Public key Signatures, key exchange: No longer secure" ((↗[55:table 1, page 2]).

Mathematical safeguards against the attacks of quantum computers, as well as programming of software that can do this, as well as the special need for secure online communication on the Internet today, require a fundamentally different view on encryption algorithms than they did in the nineteenth century or even at the beginning of the twentieth century.

The approaching end of the life cycle of the RSA algorithm therefore requires programming alternatives into existing software products to save the patient "PKI" from death by transplantation. Or, concretely, to save the XMPP clients with RSA from decay.

Programs that exclusively offer the RSA algorithm have now reached the end of the product life cycle and should no longer be used!

At the same time, there are already very elaborate code and programming bases both within the applications and as a library, both in Java programming (e.g., Smoke Android Mobile Messenger) and in the C ++ programming language (e.g., Spot-On Encryption Suite) - and open source.

Another example is the library McNoodle (↗[51]), which provides the algorithm McEliece open source for C ++ and in Smoke Messenger the code in the Java language.

Source-open implementations of the McEliece algorithm in Java and C++ messenger applications therefore served as model projects, which were to be taken up in research and teaching and are also described here as early indicators of a Transformation of Cryptography.

Cryptography on mobile devices (24)

Finally, the cryptography in the Internet age has changed dramatically with mobile devices: the smartphone seems to be stuck in the purse or in the pocket of each jeans - at least on the way out of the house. Computers in everyone's pocket now encrypt our online communications over the network.

Only a few technologies (such as the car, a heater, or the television) have reached the population just as comprehensively as the Internet and the smartphone. In both areas, privacy and, hence, the foundations of Human Rights (↗[17][41][70]) are protected by technical encryption (and not by a written policy in addition): Encrypting technology should now be created especially on the mobile smartphones.

Effects of cryptographic developments on education policy and its nomenclatura

---

As in every subject area, there is also a vocabulary of technical terms in mathematics and cryptography.

These more than two dozen groundbreaking developments and innovations are each worth a detailed study on their own - hence this in combination: What a necessary impulse to adapt the conceptual world to modern times and to further deepen, compare, and network it with extensive research.

Further examples of an urgent need to update the curriculums, terms and nomenclatura are, for example, technical research results or new standards agreed in committees: For example, TwoFish has become ThreeFish, instead of SSL we now speak of TLS in new versions or SHA-1 has become SHA-3 converted.

Information sent over the Internet is largely protected by encryption; because they are increasingly also consciously collected by third parties for evaluations, or even tapped, in order to crack them or to tap them by appropriate techniques or in processes with gaps. Here it is important to exclude security gaps by outdated standards.

In addition to the numerous proprietary applications and applications before 2010, elaborate messaging projects such as RetroShare, Spot-On and GoldBug as well as various mobile device messengers such as Conversations, Delta Chat or Smoke Chat and others (↗ also the Messenger Scorecards [03:32] & [23:100]) democratizes the encryption of the mobile and online communication of citizens with its open source code.

But already two decades after the introduction of the Internet, or a decade after the introduction of the smartphone and the establishment of the currently dominant mobile operating system

Android and the corresponding developments of technological protection of content and the communication of computers and mobile devices via the Internet may be due to the rapid development in the IT sector also the half-life of knowledge in the field of cryptography might already be more than 50 percent: It is therefore not wrong to learn, renew, and continuously update this knowledge.

The described developments, innovations, and new applications in cryptography not only influence programming, the professional world with its business processes or an open source community, but in particular the shifting educational processes have to keep pace with this development and Transformation of Cryptography.

Extensive education and training processes in the field of modern cryptography and Internet security with the inclusion of neighboring disciplines are more important than ever today. Thus, this discipline is interdisciplinary and requires an interdisciplinary discourse.

To conclude this essay, let us take three innovative processes and developments in the field of encryption in an exemplary summary once again with regard to the future design of curricula: Basic concepts such as secure end-to-end encryption, or even the deniability of keys in forward secrecy, have now been extended by new concepts and process innovations. A user today can not only use a session-based key, but also renew it with Cryptographic Calling at any time using different methods of "Cryptographic Calling" for secure end-to-end encryption: IPFS - Instant Perfect Forward Secrecy.

Fiasco Forwarding sends a dozen keys for decoding a chat message in the sense of a volatile encryption.

Even more: Machines and network nodes learn adaptively through the "Cryptographic Discovery"; new protocols (such as the POPTASTIC protocol, the Echo Protocol or the Vapor Protocol) and cryptographic matching develop a new understanding of routing: Namely, a "Beyond Cryptographic Routing" also in the context of network and graph theory.

So routing is no longer cryptographic routing, but routing has emancipated itself and quasi abolished itself to a state of "Beyond Cryptographic Routing": If the graph theory and network theory is added to cryptography, it can be found in Mesh- and Flooding-Networks such as an Echo Network and Exponential Encryption.

Open Source libraries, such as the McNoodle library for the McEliece algorithm, democratizes encryption even in the age of (post-) quantum cryptography and replaces the RSA algorithm.

The specialist area and faculty is therefore (in) a major transformation: Not only algorithms are dying, but also new developments, processes and innovations are shaping new paths and applications.

As the years go by, new curricula and learning requirements will arise that will not only require a trainer who has gone through such a school to perform, for example, a mathematical calculation, but possibly also to create a programming or application in a self-programmed application, up to network administrations for an appropriate server-client infrastructure.

All this will require not only a strengthening of interdisciplinary centers, but also regional global networks - both in the personal and in the networking of software and departments over the Internet.

In order to stem this in the future, to integrate these transformations and interdisciplinary concepts into our educational processes, it requires as an initial start a greater awareness of the current nomenclatura and a learning of the basic vocabulary and facts in cryptography and related disciplines.

So far, however, many of these subjects are in the education of many still a niche and special discipline, which is reserved in mathematics or in learning an applied programming. There are numerous contents that are worth knowing and also fascinating and can be fun.

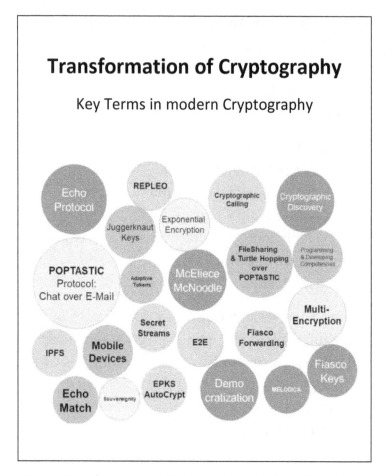

Transformation of Cryptography

Key Terms in modern Cryptography

Figure: Transformation of Cryptography - Key-terms in modern Cryptography

The goal must therefore be to transfer the expert knowledge on cryptography into broader general knowledge. This begins with getting to know individual vocabulary, their definitions as well as content and processes:

Reading material for students must therefore be continuously updated and/or redefined: In addition to the learners, teachers and multipliers also play a decisive role in the transfer of knowledge.

Therefore, exercises could be documented, which can give suggestions for a design of lessons, e.g. with the game for teaching "Cryptographic Cafeteria" (in: ↗ [56]), in which students prepare a presentation on by random chosen topics.

Outlook: Further Democratization of Encryption through Dialogue & Open Source

As already hinted at the beginning: The Transformation of Cryptography does not take place only with the described technical contents, but also with the extension of the recipient of the contents. And third, with a source-open design of the transfer.

The knowledge of the methods of encryption has reached in concentric circles more layers and knowledge carriers: It is a development from the experts of state and military institutions as knowledge carriers of cryptographic processes to scholars and students at universities and colleges as knowledge carriers to nowadays to the individuals who create encryption in companies for customers, users and the market, or learn about it in school lessons.

The "Democratization of Cryptography" (↗[[23]]) has therefore given knowledge and experience in the Internet age to even more groups: Consultancies and actors in the many institutions of the world dealing with sensitive and protected data: They can be found e.g. in the financial world, healthcare, public and academic institutions, human rights groups, non-governmental organizations, the entertainment industry, and any open source community.

No longer political and military protectors and observers of secrets and their procedures, but mathematicians and computer scientists had and have the human right to privacy through a calculation of the truth as strong as never before in the hand.

Added to this are users of open source encryption programs that describe these in a generally understandable way for others.

In the meantime, every citizen can cryptographically secure communication and content to be transferred by programming their own software with appropriate code libraries, frameworks and compilers. With open source libraries and applications, encryption has taken a promising and necessary route among users of the Internet.

In the future, the three topics "Going-The-Extra-Mile" and the use of "Virtual Keyboard" as well as works in the sense of "Open Source" - with regard to cryptographic software, but also in regards of texts, as they e.g. can be found in Wikipedia – will develop further ($\nearrow$[56]).

Since the encryption should not be broken or provided with back-doors, it remains only to tap the text inputs before the encryption process.

This is done on devices that have another "layer" - not to say Trojan horse - with which the written texts can be intercepted. Therefore, it is important to design the input and then encryption of text on devices that have never been on the Internet, so there is no chance that they will have a tap interface via online injection, or even text on the keyboard of the operating system could be sent unnoticed in an existing online connection to third parties.

The term "Going the Extra Mile" points to this "last mile" to a terminal that is not connected to the Internet, but can still pass the encrypted packet to a device (for example, via Bluetooth), which then performs the shipping in the regular online network.

Furthermore, a virgin device of the "Extra Mile" also offers the option that the file containing the private key cannot easily be uploaded by attackers and encrypted text can then be converted together with the private and public key, thanks to an obtained copy of the private key from a defined storage path of the device connected to the Internet.

And second: "Virtual Keyboards", that are keyboards that are in the same process as the actual application (e.g. the text messenger) also provide greater security than keyboards of the operating systems that could be infected or branch off text.

Third: In the future, open source cryptographic software will not only be integrated into the teaching process, but its use will also be described online and thus available for every citizen.

And this might be a Social Transformation of Cryptography, as it is driven by the Open Source Community and the Citizens.

References

[01]   Abdalla, Michel / Lange, Tanja (2012): Pairing-based cryptography - Pairing 2012, 5th International Conference, Cologne, Germany, May 16-18.

[02]   Adams, Carlisle / Lloyd, Steve (2003): Understanding PKI: concepts, standards, and deployment considerations, Addison-Wesley Professional, pp. 11–15.

[03]   Adams, David / Maier, Ann-Kathrin (2016): BIG SEVEN Study, open source crypto-messengers to be compared - or: Comprehensive Confidentiality Review & Audit of GoldBug, Encrypting E-Mail-Client & Secure Instant Messenger, Descriptions, tests and analysis reviews of 20 functions of the application GoldBug based on the essential fields and methods of evaluation of the 8 major international audit manuals for IT security investigations including 38 figures and 87 tables.,   URL: https://sf.net/projects/goldbug/files/bigseven -crypto-audit.pdf - English / German Language, Version 1.1, 305 pages, June.

[04]   Ayushi (2010): A Symmetric Key Cryptographic Algorithm, International Journal of Computer Applications, s 1(14):1–4, February.

[05]   Ben-Or, Michael / et. al. (1990): Everything provable is provable in zero-knowledge; in: Goldwasser, S. (Ed.): Advances in Cryptology—CRYPTO '88, Lecture Notes in Computer Science, 403, Springer, pp. 37–56.

[06]   Bernstein, Daniel J. (2010): Grover vs. McEliece, URL: http://cr.yp.to/codes/grovercode-20100303.pdf.

[07]   Biham, Eli / Shamir, Adi (1996): The next Stage of Differential Fault Analysis: How to break completely unknown cryptosystems.

[08]   Black, Michael (2013): When I first heard of GoldBug - Review of GoldBug Secure Instant Messenger, URL: http://www.lancedoma.ru/, 29 Oct.

[09]   Blum, Manuel / Feldman, Paul / Micali, Silvio (1988): Non-Interactive Zero-Knowledge and Its Applications, Proceedings of the Twentieth Annual ACM Symposium on Theory of Computing (STOC 1988), pp. 103–112.

[10]   Boudot, Fabrice / Schoenmakers, Berry / Traoré, Jacques (2001): A Fair and Efficient Solution to the Socialist Millionaires' Problem, Discrete Applied Mathematics, 111 (1), pp. 23-36.

[11]   Buktu, Tim (2013): NTRU: Quantum-Resistant cryptography, Independent / not affiliated with NTRU Cryptosystems, Inc.

[12]   Calderbank, Michael (2007): The RSA Cryptosystem:
        History, Algorithm, Primes.

[13]   Cohn-Gordon, Katriel / et al. (2016): A Formal
        Security Analysis of the Signal Messaging
        Protocol, Cryptology ePrint Archive, IACR).

[14]   Cremers, Cas / Feltz, Michèle (2015): Beyond eCK:
        perfect forward secrecy under actor
        compromise and ephemeral-key reveal,
        Designs, Codes and Cryptography, 74 (1): 183–
        218.

[15]   Daemen, Joan / Rijmen, Vincent (2011): The design of
        Rijndael - AES - The Advanced Encryption
        Standard, Springer, Berlin, London.

[16]   Delfs, Hans / Knebl, Helmut (2007): Symmetric-key
        encryption, Introduction to cryptography:
        principles and applications, Springer.

[17]   Delgado-Bonal, Alfonso / Martín-Torres, Javier
        (2016): Human vision is determined based on
        information theory, Scientific Reports, 6 (1).

[18]   Diffie, Whitfield / Hellman, Martin (1976): New
        directions in cryptography, 22, IEEE
        transactions on Information Theory, p. 644-
        654.

[19]   Diffie, Whitfield / van Oorschot, Paul C. / Wiener,
        Michael J. (1992): Authentication and
        Authenticated Key Exchanges, Designs, Codes
        and Cryptography,2(2):107–125

[20]   Dinh, Hang / Moore, Cristopher / Russell, Alexander / Rogaway, Philip (Ed.) (2011): McEliece and Niederreiter cryptosystems that resist quantum Fourier sampling attacks, Advances in cryptology—CRYPTO 2011, Lecture Notes in Computer Science, 6841, Heidelberg, pp. 761–779.

[21]   Dobbertin, Hans / Rijmen, Vincent / Sowa, Aleksandra (Eds.) (2005): Advanced Encryption Standard - AES - 4th international conference, AES 2004, Bonn, Germany, May 10-12, 2004: revised selected and invited papers, Springer, Berlin.

[22]   Dragomir, Mircea (2016): GoldBug Instant Messenger - Softpedia Review: This is a secure P2P Instant Messenger that ensures private communication based on a multi encryption technology constituted of several security layers,   URL: http://www.softpedia.com/get/Internet/Chat /Instant-Messaging/GoldBug-Instant-Messenger.shtml, Softpedia Review, January 31st.

[23]   Edwards, Scott / Spot-On.sf.net Project (Eds.) (2019): Communicating like dolphins with Spot-On Encryption Suite: Democratization of Multiple & Exponential Encryption; Handbook and User Manual as practical software guide with introductions   into   Cryptography,

Cryptographic Calling and Cryptographic Discovery, P2P Networking, Graph-Theory, NTRU, McEliece, the Echo Protocol and the Spot-On Software, ISBN 9783749435067, Norderstedt.

[24] EFF (2016): End-to-End Encryption, EFF Surveillance Self-Defence Guide, Electronic Frontier Foundation.

[25] EuroPKI (2010): Public key infrastructures, services and applications: 7th European workshop, EuroPKI 2010, Athens, Greece, September 23 - 24.

[26] Even S. / Goldreich, O. (1985): On the power of cascade ciphers, ACM Transactions on Computer Systems, vol. 3, pp. 108–116.

[27] Floyd, S. / Fall, K. (1999): Promoting the Use of End-to-End Congestion Control in the Internet (IEEE/ACM Transactions on Networking, August).

[28] Gadimov, Bahtiar (2015): Initial OMEMO commit, dev.gajim.org.

[29] Gaines, Helen F. (2014): Cryptanalysis - A Study of Ciphers and Their Solution, Courier Corporation.

[30] Gasakis, Mele / Schmidt, Max (2018): Beyond Cryptographic Routing: The Echo Protocol in the new Era of Exponential Encryption (EEE) -

A comprehensive essay about the Sprinkling Effect of Cryptographic Echo Discovery (SECRED) and further innovations in cryptography around the Echo Applications Smoke, SmokeStack, Spot-On, Lettera and GoldBug Crypto Chat Messenger addressing Encryption, Graph-Theory, Routing and the change from Mix-Networks like Tor or I2P to Peer-to-Peer-Flooding-Networks like the Echo respective to Friend-to-Friend Trust-Networks like they are built over the POPTASTIC protocol, ISBN 978-3-7481-5198-2, Norderstedt.

[31]   Goldberg, Ian / Stedman, Ryan / Yoshida. Kayo (2008): A User Study of Off-the-Record Messaging, University of Waterloo, Symposium on Usable Privacy and Security (SOUPS) 2008, July 23–25, Pittsburgh, PA, USA, URL: http://www.cypherpunks.ca/~iang/pubs/otr_userstudy.pdf, & URL: https://otr.cypherpunks.ca/Protocol-v3-4.0.0.html.

[32]   Gultsch, Daniel (2018): Federated Instant Messaging with Jabber/XMPP - FOSSASIA 2018, published 25.03.2018, Min: 8:55, outdated XMPP servers: jabber.systemausfall.org, jabber.hot-chilli.net, elaon.de, jabber.fr, jabber.de, high-way.me, bommboo.de, mail.de; URL:

https://www.youtube.com/watch?v=5pJYGQ_
oKks

[33] Hao, F. / Ryan, P. (2019): J-PAKE - Authenticated Key
      Exchange Without PKI, Springer Transactions
      on Computational Science XI, Special Issue on
      Security in Computing, Part II, Vol. 6480, pp.
      192-206.

[34] Harvey, Cynthia / Datamation (2015): 50 Noteworthy
      Open Source Projects – Chapter Secure
      Communication: GoldBug Messenger ranked
      on first # 1 position for Secure
      Communication,   URL:
      http://www.datamation.com/open-
      source/50-noteworthy-new-open-source-
      projects-3.html, posted September 19.

[35] Hildenbrand, Jerry (2016): Everyone is a node: How
      Wi-Fi Mesh Networking work, URL:
      https://www.androidcentral.com/how-wifi-
      mesh-networks-work.

[36] Hoffstein, Jeffrey / Pipher, Jill / Silverman, Joseph H.
      (1998): NTRU - A ring-based public key
      cryptosystem, Algorithmic Number Theory,
      Lecture Notes in Computer Science, 1423, pp.
      267–288.

[37] Honda, Osamu / Ohsaki, Hiroyuki / Imase, Makoto /
      Ishizuka, Mika / Murayama, Junichi (2005):
      Understanding TCP over TCP: effects of TCP

tunneling on end-to-end throughput and latency.

[38] Houmkozlis, Christos N. / Rovithakis, George A. (2012): End-to-end adaptive congestion control in TCP/IP networks; in: Automation and control engineering series, CRC Press, Boca Raton, Fla.

[39] Huang, Yahsin (2019): Decentralized Public Key Infrastructure (DPKI): What is it and why does it matter?, Hacker Noon.

[40] Informationweek (2016): Google's Cloud Lets You Bring customer-supplied encryption keys (CSEK), URL: http://www.informationweek.com/cloud/infr astructure-as-a-service/googles-cloud-lets-you-bring-your-own-encryption-keys/d/d-id/1326482.

[41] Joint Committee on Human Rights (2007): Government response to the Committee's fourteenth report of session 2007-08, Data protection and human rights - twenty-second report of session 2007-08, report, together with formal minutes, and an appendix.

[42] Joos, Thomas (2014): Sicheres Messaging im Web, URL: http://www.pcwelt.de/ratgeber/ Tor__I2p__Gnunet__RetroShare__Freenet__ GoldBug__Spurlos_im_Web-

Anonymisierungsnetzwerke-8921663.html, PCWelt Magazin, 01. Oktober.

[43] Joux, Antoine (2009): Algorithmic Cryptanalysis, CRC Press.

[44] Katz, Jonathan (2015): Public-key cryptography - PKC 2015 : 18th IACR International Conference on Practice and Theory in Public-Key Cryptography, Springer, Gaithersburg, MD, USA, March 30 - April 1.

[45] Kerckhoffs, Auguste (1883): La cryptographie militaire, Journal des sciences militaires, vol. IX, pp. 5–83, January 1883, pp. 161–191.

[46] Lindner, Mirko (2014): POPTASTIC: Verschlüsselter Chat über POP3 mit dem GoldBug Messenger, Pro-Linux, URL: http://www.pro-linux.de/news/1/21822/poptastic-verschluesselter-chat-ueber-pop3.html, 9. Dezember.

[47] Marlinspike, Moxie (2013): Advanced cryptographic ratcheting, Signal Blog, November 26.

[48] Matejka, Petr (2004): Model of Turtle network - Security in Peer-to-Peer Networks, Master Thesis. URL: http://turtle-p2p.sourceforge.net/thesis2.pdf.

[49] Maurer, M. / Massey, J. L. (1993): Cascade ciphers - The importance of being first, Journal of Cryptology, vol. 6, no. 1, pp. 55–61.

[50]   McEliece, Robert J. (1978): A Public-Key Cryptosystem Based On Algebraic Coding Theory, DSN Progress Report. 44: 114–116.

[51]   McNoodle Library (2016): Implementation of the McEliece Algorithm in C++, Github.

[52]   Mermin, David (2006): Breaking RSA Encryption with a Quantum Computer: Shor's Factoring Algorithm, Cornell University, Physics, 481-681.

[53]   Modadugu, Nagendra / Rescorla, Eric (2003): The Design and Implementation of Datagram TLS, Stanford Crypto Group.

[54]   NIST (2001): Announcing the ADVANCED ENCRYPTION STANDARD (AES), Federal Information Processing Standards Publication 197. United States National Institute of Standards and Technology (NIST), URL: http://nvlpubs.nist.gov/nistpubs/FIPS/NIST.FIPS.197.pdf, November 26.

[55]   NIST / Chen, Lily / Jordan, Stephen / Liu, Yi-Kai / Moody, Dustin / Peralta, Rene / Perlner, Ray / Smith-Tone, Daniel (2016): NISTIR 8105, DRAFT, Report on Post-Quantum Cryptography, URL: http://csrc.nist.gov/publications/drafts/nistir-8105/nistir_8105_draft.pdf, National Institute of Standards and Technology. February.

[56]   Nomenclatura (2019): Encyclopedia of modern Cryptography and Internet Security: From AutoCrypt and Exponential Encryption to Zero-Knowledge-Proof Keys, ISBN: 9783746066684.

[57]   Popescu, Bogdan C. / Crispo, Bruno / Tanenbaum, Andrew S. (2004): Safe and Private Data Sharing with Turtle: Friends Team-Up and Beat the System, in: 12th International Workshop on Security Protocols, Cambridge, UK, April.URL: http://turtle-P2P.sourceforge.net/turtleinitial.pdf.

[58]   Possony Stefan T. (2013): Zur Bewältigung der Kriegsschuldfrage: Völkerrecht und Strategie bei der Auslösung zweier Weltkriege, Berlin, p. 204.

[59]   Qt Digia (2015): Qt Digia has awarded GoldBug IM as reference project for Qt implementation in the official Qt-Showroom of Digia: showroom.qt-project.org/goldbug/.

[60]   Quisquater, Jean-Jacques / Guillou, Louis C. / Berson, Thomas A. (1990): How to Explain Zero-Knowledge Protocols to Your Children, Advances in Cryptology – CRYPTO '89, 435, pp. 628–631.

[61]   Saint-Andre, Peter et. al. (2016): Manifesto: A Public Statement Regarding Ubiquitous Encryption on the XMPP Network, URL:

https://github.com/stpeter/manifesto/blob/m
aster/manifesto.txt

[62]   Sinkov, Abraham (1966): Elementary Cryptanalysis: A
       Mathematical   Approach,   Mathematical
       Association of America.

[63]   Smoke   (2017):   Documentation   of   the   Android
       Messenger   Application   Smoke   with
       Encryption,   URL:
       https://github.com/textbrowser/smoke/raw/
       master/Documentation/Smoke.pdf, 2017.

[64]   SmokeStack: Server   Software   for   Encrypted
       Messaging,   URL:
       https://github.com/textbrowser/smokestack

[65]   Spot-On   (2011):   Documentation   of   the   Spot-On-
       Application,   URL:
       https://sourceforge.net/p/spot-
       on/code/HEAD/tree/, under this URL since
       06/2013, Sourceforge, including the Spot-On:
       Documentation of the project draft paper of
       the pre-research project since 2010, Project
       Ne.R.D.D.,   Registered   2010-06-27,   URL:
       https://sourceforge.net/projects/nerdd/   has
       evolved into Spot-On. Please see http://spot-
       on.sf.net   and   URL:
       https://github.com/textbrowser/spot-
       on/blob/master/branches/Documentation/RE
       LEASE-NOTES.archived, 08.08.2011.

[66]   Spot-On (2019): Documentation of the Spot-On-Application,   URL:
        https://github.com/textbrowser/spot-on/tree/master/
        branches/trunk/Documentation, Github 2019.

[67]   Stehlé, Damien / Steinfeld, Ron (2016): Making
        NTRUEncrypt and NTRUSign as Secure as
        Standard Worst-Case Problems over Ideal
        Lattices, Cryptology ePrint Archive.

[68]   Stevens, W. Richard (1996): TCP/IP Illustrated,
        Volume 3: TCP for Transactions, HTTP, NNTP,
        and the UNIX Domain Protocols.

[69]   Straub, Andreas (2016): XEP-0384: OMEMO
        Encryption, XMPP Standards Foundation
        website.

[70]   The United Nations / Office of the High
        Commissioner of Human Rights (2014): What
        are human rights?.

[71]   Thomas, Stephen A. (2000): SSL and TLS essentials
        securing the Web, New York: Wiley.

[72]   Tur, Henryk / Computerworld (2018): GoldBug Secure
        Email Client & Instant Messenger,
        https://www.computerworld.pl/ftp/goldbug-secure-email-Client-instant-messenger.html,
        January 11.

[73]   Urdaneta, Guido / Pierre, Guillaume / van Steen, Maarten (2011): A Survey of DHT Security Techniques, ACM Computing Surveys 43(2).

[74]   Yao, Andrew (1982): Protocols for secure communications, Proc. 23rd IEEE Symposium on Foundations of Computer Science (FOCS '82), pp. 160–164.

Linda A. Bertram
Gunther van Dooble
et al. *Editors*

Nomenclatura -

**Encyclopedia of
modern Cryptography
and Internet Security**

From AutoCrypt and Exponential Encryption
to Zero-Knowledge-Proof Keys

Hardcover: ISBN: 9783748191513

Softcover: ISBN: 9783746066684